WILL SMITH LIFE STORY

THE LIFE ACCOUNT OF WILL SMITH

STARWORLD PRESS

TABLE OF CONTENTS

BACKGROUND

With and amazing achievement in different fields of entertainment, **Will Smith** stands apart as fascinating rare gem. From the outset, before the age of 20, Smith attained fame as a rap star at going before cutting his chops as a top performer in the Hollywood with different onscreen appearances in various seasons of the years. Unequivocally today, we all know **Smith** to have an attractiveness and extreme charm for a huge number of people who love entertainment. Who doesn't love to be entertained?

From the beginning, Willard Carroll Smith, Jr. (**Will Smith**) became an American performer and entertainer whose force of character, perfect and clean incredible looks joined together with his quick psyche and helped him in changing from rap music to another productive calling in acting. To this end, he has had a great time of accomplishments in TV, film and music.

Will always wanted to pursue his life in the entertainment industry and wasn't enthused about continuing with his academics regardless of his high-grade performance in school. With his talent at hand, WILL, after completing high school, purportedly refused to look up to a chance to study in the Massachusetts Institute of Technology. **Will** and his gifts, made the world to see a beautiful transformation, from wave-making rapper to topnotch Hollywood star. Today, while we can recall his role on 'THE FRESH PRINCE OF BEL-AIR,' the dullest memory can equally count WILL's progress in different films such as INDEPENDENCE DAY,' 'MEN IN BLACK' and any semblance of 'ALI.'

Will Smith, has by balance of consistent effort and powerful allure, found fame and love in in the entertainment world today. Smith has tracked down some colossal accomplishment in two great fields of this entertainment world. As a young man, he conveyed a couple of platinum rap assortments and won the absolute first Grammy Award given in the rap class. Truly, that was an uncommon start for exquisite Smith!

With his accomplishment in the music business behind him, Smith moved to TV. During the 1990s, while still a young person by any standards, Smith was famous for TV and film occupations. Some of these new opportunities really tested his acting capacity and showed the world a clear distinction in his talent. Veronica Chambers, who was a Premiere magazine supporter, alluded to Smith for his white-bread offer that not a lot of individuals of his race have.

For Smith, acting has consistently inferred being his own specific self before a camera. He has locked in overtime to place some reality into the career and show it in his films. Looking at what the name *Fresh Prince* addresses,

Smith uncovered a picture of metropolitan youth, and most unequivocally, of Black youth. The accomplishment that followed the TV series made Will to joyfully explore the deeply, the world of entertainment. This isn't a story of a talented actor who searched for opportunities, but a multi-gifted youth with the yearning to be the best performer in the film industry. For this, he focused on all of the mind blowing credits of the blockbusters of the time. For 1993, he participated in MADE IN AMERICA and SIX DEGREES OF SEPARATION. Before long, one of his stunning positions was in the hour of 1995, when co-highlighting in BAD BOYS. Today, Will's passion, effort and consistency has not only created a beautiful memory in the hearts of fans, but has stood him out as an A-lister in the entertainment world.

SECTION ONE

EARLY LIFE

On the year 1968, 25th of September to be exact, Smith was brought into the world in a home in Philadelphia, Pennsylvania. His mother Caroline, was into education, and his father Willard C. Smith, was an owner of a company that focused on refrigeration. Smith had a Baptist life at home, yet acknowledged his tutoring from a Catholic school 'Our Lady of Lourdes'. He attended Overbrook High School in Philadelphia and there, his teachers nicknamed him "THE PRINCE" since they felt he was so charming. His best subject was math, and he secured sufficient grades to be recognized at the regarded Massachusetts Institute of Technology. By then, in any case, fate had proclaimed another way for the PRINCE. How about his parents? Will spoke about his dad and mom has being revering but also motivating, the sort of parents who took their young son to Mount Rushmore to show that academic guidance doesn't end in homeroom of schools.

In Will's disposition, the father kept him in line, however he was extreme, but he was not overbearing. The dad could also make his money from fixing refrigeration in corner stores and reliably obliged the family. **Will** made it known that his father showed up as steady and positive figure in his incredible life. What's more with regards to the Mom? She worked as a school secretary and her ways were that of academic instruction. While feeling he went to a Catholic school since it was the best school nearby, WILL in like manner felt a part of the leaders and nuns showed some level of racism.

His West Philadelphia region was a combination of social orders where Orthodox Jews lived along with Muslim people. Smith was a good understudy whose boggling character and quick tongue were renowned for getting him free.

At age 12, Smith began rapping, mirroring legends like Grandmaster Flash. Notwithstanding, he touched his rhymes with a comedic part that later transform into a piece of his music style. At 16, Smith met Jeff Townes at a party. The pair became friends, and the group DJ Jazzy Jeff and The Fresh Prince was born.

FAMILY

With Smith Sr, Willard Carroll as father and Bright, Caroline as mother, Smith had three kin: Pam, Ellen and Harry. In May, 1992, he grew up to wed his first spouse, brought forth one kid, and separated in December 1995. In 1997, he got hitched to Jada Pinkett and they brought forth two youngsters. Altogether, Smith is presently a dad of three: Jaden, Willow and Trey.

INDIVIDUAL LIFE

As time could make him see more of life at a young age, his father and mother actually separated when he was 13. Unfortunately, finally ended the marriage when Will Smith was 32. Smith conceded that he considered implosion after his mother Caroline Bright who was really mauled by the father, left her family. Explaining the conditions under which the mother left, the performer said that she'd had enough of his father's abuse. Smith said the event left him feeling ruined and repentant, and drove him to pointless thoughts.

Smith has been hitched twice. His first marriage, to Sheree Zampino in 1992, persevered through only three years and gave birth to "**Trey**." Later in 1997, got married to Jada Pinkett Smith. In 1998, they brought forth **Jaden**. In 2000, **Willow** arrived to make it a family of three children for Smith.

Although Will Smith shows up politically liberal, he upheld the political effort of previous president Barack Obama. Smith gave $4,600 to this course. Smith is an enthusiast of chess and PC games. He loves to take his mother on vacations to Arizona. His Nicknames Include: Will, Fresh Prince and Mr. July.

WILL has focused his review on different religions, including Scientology, and he has expressed various free opinions about Scientology and various convictions. In any case, Smith thinks a huge load of the musings in Scientology are awesome and moderate and non-severe and Ninety-eight percent of the norms in Scientology are undefined from the principles of the Bible.

He has denied having joined the Church of Scientology, saying he is a Christian, however appreciates on all religions who respect all people and all ways. After his spouse, Jada, made the film **Collateral** with Cruise in 2004, the couple gave 20,000 dollars to Scientology's Hollywood Education and Literacy Program, which is the a major base for Scientology's self-instructing structure.

MARITAL LIFE

Smith, who portrayed himself as a one-woman man, got married to Sheree Zampino in 1992. The marriage saw "Trey," their first child arriving the following year. Trey featured in his father's music video for the 1998 single "JUST THE TWO OF US." Talking about his first wife, Smith said he comprehended that really, genuinely and intellectually she was on a higher plane than him. Smith portrayed her as amazing woman who allowed him to finally put down the sacks of energetic strain he had been hauling near.

From every one of these, we might say Smith's life gave off an impression of being absolutely marvelous perfect. Indeed! He was a rapper, TV star, life partner, father, and a sprouting well known entertainer. Notwithstanding, his marriage was on a smooth and unpleasant path. His life partner, Sheree Zampino in a little while mentioned divorce and it was closed in 1995. The two of them share guardianship of their kid. Anyway, despite the situation, Smith continued with his TV, rap, and film livelihoods.

On the run, Smith met Jada Pinkett when she went for a task on THE FRESH PRINCE OF BEL AIR, later thy got related with one another. On the 31st December, 1997, they were joined in marriage. Smith conveyed that Jada is the essential individual he has been with, who was prepared to recognize that it's not ceaselessly going to be unprecedented, but simultaneously that is OK. Of late, the 53-year-old performer which has been hitched for a long while to Jada Pinkett Smith asserted that the two are in an open marriage. He admitted they managed against monogamy since they were both sad and clearly something expected to change. This followed basic limitless discussions about, what is social faultlessness and what is the best technique for discussing as a partner. Furthermore, for the huge piece of the relationship, monogamy was what WILL and JADA picked, this doesn't mean they considered monogamy the vitally friendly perfection. Nonetheless, as of now, they have offered each other trust and chance, with the conviction that everybody needs to find their own particular way. Likewise, marriage for them can't be a prison.

Will Smith and Jada Pinkett Smith have maybe the longest marriage in Hollywood following getting the pack in 1997, yet their opinion has been far from plain cruising. Resulting to having two kids, they momentarily went their separate ways in 2011, and returned together after the Smith has some sex talk with a counselor. The couple appeared to have participated in a particularly powerful sexual concurrence when they at first began dating after he isolated from first life partner Sheree Zampino in 1995, and eventually continued to wed in 1997 when Jada was three months pregnant with kid Jaden.

Will revealed he and Jada were in the agonies of excitement for quite a while, drank every day, and occupied with sexual relations on various events every day, for four straight months and it made him continue to ponder whether it was a test. In any case, taking everything into account, there were only two possibilities. It was conceivably he satisfies the woman truly or he fails miserably endeavoring to. From this, plainly he and Jada were blown in intimacy right from the beginning. Without a doubt, it ended up being altogether more confounding than that. WILL once explained that he and Jada are great on conversations, are as yet joined and are not choking the life out of each other because they can manage their issues. He agreed he has recently never met another person that he can connect with in conversation more euphorically and helpfully than Jada. Despite this, their dream relationship hasn't been so plain cruising.

MORE TO KNOW

Will Smith uncovered up extra concerning his relationship with his partner in a scene with The Oprah Conversation. The performer uncovers how his relationship with Jada made after they began dating in 1995. As his first marriage arrived at a divorce, Will and Jada had a significant affiliation, one that has continued for more than twenty years. For sure, even after they got marriage in 1997, Will and Jada never had a married customarily.

They had a relationship that bright lights on connection as opposing the prison type of relationship. At one point, they even headed out in different directions. In WILL's opening, they never fully disengaged. What happened was they perceived that it was fantasy duplicity that they could make each other happy. They agreed that they expected to satisfy themselves in their various ways, and thereafter, acquaint themselves back with the relationship happily. This was their technique as against mentioning that one individual fills an empty cup of the other. They made plans to a finish of figuring out specific ways of being content. To WILL, that time isolated helped them with tracking down the power of adoring uninhibitedly. That opportunity has inferred extramarital associations for both Will and Jada; notwithstanding, this doesn't intend to be a thing which they need to stow away from the other. This was an extraordinary journey to decontaminate the poisonous, cold bits of their spirits. The significant journey was to find satisfaction and delight without 'vampirically' burning-through others. The journey is finding that happiness without remedy and interference.

THE WILL'S POWER

Smith's high confidence in himself, helped him with bouncing from neighborhood fame to public genius while still an adolescent. As the skilled Smith would see it of himself, Confidence is what stands him out. He is such a man who reliably goes through difficulties, however stocks in a choice that could be more hazardous than himself, valiant! From where may the self-conviction come from? Smith spread the word about it, that he was raised by his people to believe in the power and acknowledge it has his prosperity on a major level. Furthermore, with this, one thing Will Smith has exhibited out is a summary of various things which disperses any disarray that he has the promoting reasonability, the allure, and the capacity to utilize each possibility that come his heading.

SECTION TWO

WILL AS A MUSIC STAR

Following the name **PRINCE CHARMING** in school, he changed it to FRESH PRINCE to reflect a more hip-Hop sound when he began his rap livelihood. In 1985, when he was just 16 years old, Smith met Jeffrey Townes at a party. Townes was additionally called DJ Jazzy Jeff, and despite the way that he was two or three years more settled than Smith, he was accustomed to turning records at occasions for a significant length of time. The preview of meeting DJ Jazzy "Townes," mixed more oil of progress into Will's way. Townes was setting up a party close to Smith's home, and he was feeling the deficiency of his publicity man. Will sought after this entryway and had a significant effect that day. After this event, both became remarkable together, incredible companions and started mixing their gifts. They made a group of two called DJ Jazzy Jeff and the Fresh Prince. They began conveying music at this point kept away from the gangsta rap sound that was coming from the West Coast.

Truly, on focusing on their music, you would verify that DJ JAZZY JEFF and THE FRESH PRINCE were carried into the world with Smith dealing with the rhymes and Townes managing the power of mixing the sound. The mix was just a cool pop and hip-skip hit during the last piece of the 1980s and mid-1990s.

The Fresh Prince rapped about secondary school interruptions in an ideal, berate freestyle that Middle America found cool and locking in. In 1986, the group conveyed their first single, GIRLS AIN'T NOTHING BUT TROUBLE. Without avoiding the real issue, this was definitely a hit that year and after.

Their first collection in 1987, ROCK THE HOUSE, hit the Billboard Top 200, and made Smith a cash magnate before the age of 18. Smith's exhibit, famous for its wide half breed appeal, was every so often depicted as "light rap" because of the shortfall of straightforward stanzas and subjects in his pieces.

The social occasion acknowledged their first Grammy Award for Best Rap Performance in 1989 for PARENTS JUST DON'T UNDERSTAND. Their second most notable single was "Late spring" in 1991 with which they gained their second Grammy Award and rose to number 4 of the Billboard-Hot-100.

The early accomplishment reset Smith's head. Subsequent to being prestigious all through the Philadelphia locale, they were pursued in the rest of the country as well. As the money came in, Smith had the choice to convince his people that school could stop. For sure, he obtained more than 1,000,000 dollars before he turned 20.

From the start, it was said that Smith had turned down an award to Boston's first class MIT, but Smith later scattered the tattle when he clarified that his mother had a friend who was the affirmation official at MIT, he had pretty high SAT scores and they required Black youngsters, so he doubtlessly may have gotten in. Regardless, he had no point of going to a college.

In 1988, DJ Jazzy Jeff and The Fresh Prince continued with their success with the assortment HE'S THE DJ, I'M THE RAPPER. The album got them another success as they grabbed their first Grammy Award for Best Rap Performance. This was the first Grammy presented in the rap class. It was preceded in 1989 by AND IN THIS CORNER, which continued with the pair's climb to popularity.

The tenacious climb dropped the FRESH PRINCE in another influx of acting vocation. Meanwhile, Smith and Towne continued to make music, with their 1991 assortment HOMEBASE conveying the hits. Followed through on October 12, 1993, their last assortment together, CODE RED, was striking and well known for BOOM! SHAKE THE ROOM.

Similarly in 1997, Smith conveyed his first autonomous music collection, BIG WILLIE STYLE, which fused the hit "GETTIN' JIGGY WIT IT," and he followed it two years afterward with WILLENNIUM.

Quite a while later, After 4 years of an interruption in his music, Smith continued with his recording occupation with the assortments BORN TO REIGN in 2002 and LOST AND FOUND in 2005. Nonetheless, it didn't organize with the accomplishment of his past music, it couldn't coordinate!

THE CONCEPT OF SMITH'S MUSIC

Since their subjects were basic, DJ Jazzy Jeff and the Fresh Prince were allowed the expense of more vital opportunities to play out their work. Sponsors saw less freedom for battles at their shows, so they were set up for critical show settings. For sure, even association TV bosses felt content with putting them on the air. The unblemished rap picture showed a mixed gift and blended analysis since some other rap experts censured them for ignoring bona fide issues of the blacks.

Smith's response to analysis was that he was essentially responding to his own special current situation, one that barred the weights of a wrecked family, drug abuse, or horrendous bad behavior. Before all else, following the style of the day, his raps had a restricted amount of vulgarity. Why did he choose this style? He who is truly clear dodges obscenity; that was the expressions of Will's grandma though **Will** didn't have even the remotest clue what it inferred, yet he understood he wanted the grandmother's underwriting, comparably as he really wanted his people's support.

THE MOVIE PRODUCER

Moreover, during the 21st century Smith filled in as a maker for an impressive time span. Some are those which he acted, and with his mate, Jada Pinkett Smith, he made and delivered the sitcom ALL OF US which suffered from year 2003 to year 2007. He moreover helped produce two extra films that year,

lakeview terrace and also **the secret life of bees**.

WILL AS AN ACTOR

Some Hollywood bosses saw Smith's stage presence and his ability to charm a horde of individuals. Such innumerable accounts in this manner conveyed him to the thought of TV producers. Beginning in 1990 he was free to go for little positions on The COSBY SHOW and A DIFFERENT WORLD; but he depicted himself in as being too scared to even think about keeping to the plans. Finally, he met Benny Medina who heads Warner Brothers Records.

Medina and Smith thoroughly made some thinking and thereafter advanced toward creator Quincy Jones about a pilot scene. Jones immediately distinguished that a show of that nature highlighting Will Smith would be a hit. The TV sitcom THE FRESH PRINCE OF BEL-AIR, what began in 1990, was roughly established on Smith's real image. It ran on NBC for six productive seasons, completing at the star's requesting, and during its run Smith gathered two nominations in Golden Globe Award and filled in as a central creator for the last season. The show tracked down a gathering of individuals quickly, while keeping a lot of people expectant on Monday nights.

For Smith, who had never done any acting, the show was a genuine test. He investigated that he was apprehensive while making a good endeavor, he would recall the entire role, and subsequently lip everybody's lines while they were talking. Smith likely will not have been content with his work, be that as it may, practically every other individual was.

While at this point making THE FRESH PRINCE OF BEL-AIR, in 1992, Smith wandered into film with WHERE THE DAY TAKES YOU. Furthermore to follow was a 1993 farce MADE IN AMERICA, followed by a 1993 broadly applauded lead in SIX DEGREES OF SEPARATION. This was his first lead-work, and Smith played a street smart gay who cons his course through a-list circles.

After the series got done, Smith moved from TV to film, and finally highlighted in different blockbuster films. He is the primary performer to have eight persistent films gross in excess of 100 million dollars in the local entertainment world; eleven successive films gross in excess of 150 million dollars all around just as eight consecutive movies in which he included open at the best position in the movies count.

The 1995 BAD BOYS, regardless, was another vital turning point in his film calling. The high-spending plan cop film saw him work together with comic Martin Lawrence, parting away from the Black-cop/white-cop formula that had been so productive for BEVERLY HILLS Cop and the LETHAL Weapon series. While the film was not an essential accomplishment, it made in excess of 100 million dollars all over the planet, showing star power of Smith.

In 1996 he highlighted in that year's top-netting film, INDEPENDENCE DAY. His occupation here confirmed him as a focal part in Hollywood and a top individual for summer blockbusters. He played a pilot driving the counterattack against meddling powers, and his comedic capacities handily changed into the sharp jokes all conflict legends ought to have drop while dispatching their rivals. This was an extraordinary accomplishment in his acting vocation.

He was a hit in the film world again the next year with the sci-fi spoof MEN IN BLACK. In the comparative year, Will began his presentation calling with the appearance of the mark tune for MEN IN BLACK, which got into the top places of music. It was the skilled Smith who rapped the mark melody for the film, and making it a piece of his 1997 collection, BIG WILLIE STYLE, brought the multi-gifted performer greater accomplishment.

In 1998, following including in the ENEMY OF THE STATE, Smith continued to show his uncommon adaptability as a performer. His series of hits left another engraving in 1999 with WILD WEST. Disregarding the film's poor rating in the movies, the track Smith cut for the film transformed into a hit on his 1999 music album, WILLENNIUM. Away from that, Smith proceeded to play a puzzling golf collaborator in The 2000 LEGEND OF BAGGER VANCE.

The 2001 movie, ALI, which was a portrayal of legend Muhammad Ali, showed WILL the opportunity to retake his big-screen fame. This possibility saw Smith put the presentation of his life, getting ready and limiting himself to unprecedented lengths to do value to the rawness, and mental self-view of the ostensible character. The film disillusioned in the artistic world notwithstanding a record-breaking first day of the period, but Smith's display was adequate to give him his first ACADEMY AWARD nomination.

A few continuations were immediately, with Smith rehashing his parts in MEN IN BLACK II in 2002 and BAD BOYS II In 2003. Albeit none of the work was a disappointment, none could meet with the level of its previous work. Staying with the science fiction action subject, Smith progressed forward to "I, ROBOT" in 2004. The Isaac Asimov variety included Smith as a high level cop exploring a murder by a robot and a while later captivating a robot insubordination. The film performed well, procuring more than $144 million locally.

In 2005, Smith's persuading charmer character was put to use in the 2005 HITCH, playing a dating master who helps shocking people with their emotional moves. Smith furthermore composed the tune for the film and utilized it for his 2005 music collection, LOST AND FOUND. Hitch was a huge accomplishment. The next year he highlighted in THE PURSUIT OF HAPPYNESS, and his show as a solitary parent who routs trouble gained him a second nomination for **Oscar** award in best actor.

In the 2007 film, I AM LEGEND, Smith displayed as a possibly the ever going human on Earth following scientist a pandemic and he battled savage vampires.

The film transformed into a public and worldwide hit. With amazingly certain overviews, its opening was the greatest ever for a film conveyed in the United States during December. Now, everybody realized a man like Smith is essentially exceptional.

In 2008, HANCOCK included Smith as a godlike endeavoring to re-try his hated picture. Same year, he expected a section in SEVEN POUNDS as a man searching for recovery after unexpectedly killing seven people in a car collision.

After a break, Smith returned to the big screen in 2012 with Men in Black 3, this task of his was followed by a job as a tactical forerunner in the on a very basic level panned science fiction, AFTER EARTH, which co-highlighted Smith's youngster Jaden. He then, showed up as Lucifer in the film WINTER'S TALE in 2014.

In 2015 Smith portrayed a blackmailer in the roller coaster FOCUS. That very year, he highlighted as Doctor Bennet Omalu in CONCUSSION, obtaining a Golden Globe selection for his occupation as an expert engaging to expose issues with respect to head injury in NFL players.

In 2016 he played the expert assassin deadshot in SUICIDE SQUAD and a mourning father in COLLATERAL

BEAUTY in which the individual acquiescence in a significant distress after a singular mishap. After this present, Will's father had sickness, in the end losing his battle. In the film COLLATERAL BEAUTY, Will expected to discover with respect to the great beyond and religion, and he considers this experience a wonderful technique for preparing for a film and an essentially better strategy for saying goodbye to his dad.

The following year he included as a cop in the Netflix film **BRIGHT**, which is set in a Los Angeles moved by individuals and incredible creatures. The film was appropriated by Netflix and was the most exorbitant film for the business organization.

Smith was given the genie job in the 2019 ALADDIN. In same 2019, He included in two sections in GEMINI MAN. First was as a surrendered expert assassin and his more energetic clone, the latter was as a painstakingly duplicated variation of Smith in his 20s.

Smith's various credits from 2019 works additionally recall the stimulated SPIES IN DISGUISE, where he gave the voice of a clandestine specialist who is changed into a pigeon. He then, highlighted in BAD BOYS FOR LIFE the following year. In 2021, he played the lead spot in KING

RICHARD, a film about the father of tennis stars Serena and Venus Williams.

FATHERHOOD

Will is father to Jaden, Willow, and Trey whom he had during his first association with first spouse Sheree. Smith and his youngster Jaden played father and kid in two positions: the 2006 individual show THE PURSUIT OF HAPPYNESS, and the science fiction film AFTER EARTH, which came out on 31st May, 2013.

The actor, who appeared with his kid Jaden, in AFTER EARTH, uncovered how he felt his youngster was betrayed by his exercises after he had trained him through the film. Jaden had dependably done all that WILL prepared him to do, and WILL had taught him.

However, AFTER EARTH was shocking and essential frustration, and what was more horrible was that Jaden persevered through the shot. The public responses were absolutely horrendous; they said and printed things regarding Jaden that Will Smith wouldn't repeat. WILL said they never discussed it, yet he understood he felt betrayed, deceived, and lost his trust in the father's position during that second. He at last controlled against it, but it sucks to feel like one has hurt their youngsters.

SECTION THREE

THE SMITH'S STYLE

Routinely plays a cop or a subject matter expert, as frequently as conceivable joins his appearance, AW, HELL NO! in his movies. Regularly plays defiant, leg-pulling characters; Big ears and adorable smile.

KEYNOTES ABOUT WILL

- He grew up raised as a Baptist.

- Virgo is his zodiac sign

- Will Smith has won two ACADEMY AWARDS and four GRAMMY AWARDS.

- Forbes set him as the most bankable star around the world.

- He is the sole performer with film to have progressively grosser more than $100 million in the motion pictures.

- Smith was financially weak when he had the chance to be start Fresh Prince of Bel-Air.

- His 1995 film Bad Boys, nets more than $75,600,000 abroad.

- Met first life partner, Sheree Zampino, at a taping of A DIFFERENT WORLD

- Smith married Sheree Zampino in 1992 and the marriage finished in 1995.

- He has a kid from Sheree Zampino named Willard Carroll Trey Smith all.

- Met second companion Jada Pinkett Smith when she went for a task on The Fresh Prince of Bel-Air 1990.

- He got hitched to Jada Pinkett in 1997.

- He has two children from second companion, Jaden Smith and Willow Smith.

- His youngster in Pursuit of Happiness is his authentic kid.

- In 2005, Smith was gone into the Guinness Book of World Records for going to three introductions in a 24 hour stretch.

•   His great purpose has seen him giving more than 1.3 million dollars to noble cause.

•   Appreciates playing chess.

•   As a public genuine model, worked with the Presidential Inaugural Celebration for Youth, as an element of the Gala for President Bill Clinton.

•   First hip-bounce man to be named for an Academy Award.

•   Has a record for most elevated Kids Choice Awards (6)

•   He is the second-most raised performer, behind Tom Cruise.

- October 2005, He needed to pass on his home in California on because of fierce blaze assault

- His 1995 detachment from ex Sheree Zampino provoked a $900,000 solitary sum separate from settlement for Zampino notwithstanding $24,000 every month in arrangement and child support.

- Walk 2007, went through treatment on his shoulder in a New York crisis center after he encountered a strain.

- Had a value of millions of dollars before the age of 20.

- In 2007, Forbes Magazine surveyed his pay for the year at $31 million.

- In 2004, his complete resources were surveyed to be $188 million.

- Gigantic enthusiast of wrestling.

- Is consistently called Mr July due to the manner in which an enormous piece of his mid-year blockbusters open in July.

- He has shown on live TV that he can fix a Rubik's Cube in under 55 seconds.

EARNINGS

$50,000 from the 1992 WHERE THE DAY TAKES YOU;

$100,000 from the 1993 MADE IN AMERICA;

$500,000 from the 1993　SIX DEGREES OF SEPARATION; $

2,000,000 from the 1995　BAD BOYS;

$5,000,000　from　the　1996 INDEPENDENCE DAY;

$5,000,000 from the 1997 MEN IN BLACK;

$14,000,000 from the 1998 ENEMY OF THE STATE;

$7,000,000 from the 1999 WILD WILD WEST;

$10,000,000　from　the　2000　THE LEGEND OF BAGGER VANCE;

$20,000,000 from the 2001 ALI;

$20,000,000 + from the 2002 MEN IN BLACK II;

$20,000,000 + from the 2003 BAD BOYS II;

$28,000,000 from the 2004 I, ROBOT;

$20,000,000 from the 2006 THE PURSUIT OF HAPPYNESS;

$20,000,000from the 2008 HANCOCK;

THE KARATE KID $5,500,000 +from the 2010;

$20,000,000 from the 2012 MEN IN BLACK 3;

$20 MILLION from the 2016 SUICIDE SQUAD;

$20,000,000 from the 2017 BRIGHT;

$17,000,000 from the 2020 BAD BOYS FOR LIFE

THE CASE WITH INTERNAL REVENUE SERVICE

Around 1988 and 1989, Smith went through cash but however missed the mark on his yearly assessment costs. The Internal Revenue Service over the long haul studied a $2.8 million expense commitment against Smith and took countless his resources. Smith was practically bankrupt in 1990, when the NBC TV station checked him to an arrangement and made a sitcom, The Fresh Prince of Bel-Air, around him. The show was productive and begun his acting business. Smith picked this opportunity to characterize for himself the goal of transforming into the best popular entertainer on earth. He focused on the characteristics of BOX OFFICE successes.

OTHER SOURCES OFINCOME ASIDE ACTING AND MUSIC

With over 42.7 Million allies on IG, beginning today under the username @willsmith, he secures an assessment of around 71,921 dollars to 119,868 dollars from each post through online media. Will Smith gains around 8 thousand to 128.4 thousand dollars consistently from YouTube. In case we take benefit yearly, the figures are around 96.3 thousand to 1.5 million dollars for each annum.

SUPPORTS AND INVESTMENTS

Will Smith made huge loads of money by appearing for different brands and adventures which added around 75 million to 80 million dollars consistently to his all-out resources. He has put resources into different courses like Camping App, HipCamp and esports Gen.G. In 2013, he, Jada Pinkett and Jay-Z put in 10 million dollars in Brooklyn things.

ASSETS AND WORTH

Will Smith participates in costly life and has different expensive properties under his cap which most certainly worth 100 million dollars across the world. His territory joins Kauai's North Store House which he bought for 13.5 million dollars.

CHARITY

Will Smith has successfully looked into numerous missions and has maintained diverse unselfish relationship in financial terms. In 2007, he gave 1.3 million dollars to good cause.

In 2018, he similarly went to India and played out the Hindu service of Abhisheka of Lord Shiva at Haridwar, India. He visited hallowed stream Ganga where he played out an Aarti. He said that he felt a significant relationship with Indian gem looking and Hindu.

Having said all, now and beyond, will smith will consistently be remembered as a legend with prominent mark.

Printed in Great Britain
by Amazon

39165711R00040